The Shadow of an Addict

A collection of poetry
by
Matthew Ganem

The Shadow of an Addict

A collection of poetry
by
Matthew Ganem

The Shadow of an Addict

Copyright © 2012 by Matthew Ganem

Edited by Matthew Ganem and Jasen Sousa
Book Design by Jasen Sousa

All rights reserved under international and Pan-American copyright conventions. No part of this book may be reproduced, stored in a retrieval system or transmitted in any form, electronic, mechanical, or by any other means, without written permission of the author. Address all inquiries to:

J-Rock Publishing
45 Francesca Ave
Somerville, MA 02144

Manufactured in The United States of America

Printed in Somerville, Massachusetts

This page has no correlation to the title or the contents in this collection this is for family, friends and fans to remember their fallen angels

One day standing at the cross roads
Between heaven and hell
I'll join you amongst the lost souls
When I bid this world my farewell

Joseph Ganem, Michael Ganem, Danny Nunes, James Slattery, Stephen Pacheco, Michael Sparks, Andy Collins, Ryan P. Trant, Jimmy Rava, Joshua Scott, Justin A. Canonico, Spc. Nick Peters, Brittany Peters, Meghan Gallagher, Leanne Marie Balch, Pat Daley, Joe Coiley, Mike Caissie, Steven Trentor, Robert Sousa, Michael Ciccarelli, Kyle Campbell, Paul Teves Sr., Robert L. McCluskey, Richie Maggs, David Martini, Victor J. Ferreira III, Ryan Sullivan, Matthew O'Brien, Chris Swift, Donald Slayton, Lauren Elizabeth Usher, Chris Leavitts, Daniel Thomas Johnson Jr., Spc. Jose Torre, Margaret Yoston, James Yoston, Mike Hamilton, Jessica Finned, Jarrod Porter, Ingrid Algarra, Karl Richard Cousins Jr., Frank Dillon, Dave Harris, Dave Musto, Jeff Resse, Elaine Dingle, Juana D. Acevedo Burgos Palermo, Deana Cremmin, Elliot Matos Jr., Richard Rooney, Brian Lounsbury, Adrian O'Rourke, Robert Quartarone, Michael Martinez, Frank Snow, Isabella Da Silva, Mayara Alves, Joan Miller, Lucinda J. Maitland, Dougie Fewtrell, Timothy Michael DeArmon, Donald Paul Howard, Robert Albert Owens, Richard Claflin, Brian Liberatore, Robert Dovale, Kevin Malarkey, Barbara Rogovich, Shannah Duggan, Fred Gunter, Anthony Davidson, Megan Powers, Haley Tracy Buccella, Sandra Laclair, Steven MacNeil, Emmanuel Pinto, Doowensky Nazaire, Orlando Castillo, John Michelin, Jean Marc, Romeo Murray, Chris Souza, Ian Surabian, Charlene Rosemond, Pauline Darius, Marie Mayala, Bobby Doyle, Louie Cunha, Cory Disciscio, Justin Maimaron, Michelle Ginewics, Jasen Haley, Clara Parker, Derek Matthew Eames, Nhang Nguyen, Ryan Rawson, Hilda Aurelio, Helen Molignaro, Rosa Ferreira, Antonio Nunes, Tamar Schuman, Ryan Harrington, Kenneth G O'Connell, Olivia Brianna O'Connell, Chris Ormond, Adam Culhane, Zaharoula Louloudis, Joan Batzek, Sean McDonald, Denis Mckenna, Matthew Crister, Krissy Fabiano, Rachel Doucette, Keimani Bell Sr., Chris Belloise

This book is dedicated to those without a voice, trapped in the grip of addiction, for those that still suffer from the disease, been affected by it, or are in recovery from it

TABLE OF CONTENTS

CHAPTER 1 CONFESSIONS OF A POET

The Deepest Addiction In Me	5
My Story Has To Be Told	6
I Have Your New Addiction	8
A Masked Bandits Remorse	10
The Pen Is My Sword	12
Picture Me	14
Negativity	17

CHAPTER 2 BEHIND MY DEEPEST SCAR

Night Terrors	20
An OxyContin Relapse	22
My Brown Lady Disease	24
Ripples Of The Past	27
For their sake	29
My Gateway To Heroin	30
Overdose	31
Recovery's Disciple	32
You Gave Me Better Days	35

Chapter 3 The Prison Inside My Heart

My Cards On The Table	38
Under The Man On The Moon	39
Cuts In My Broken Heart	40
Falling Into Fantasies	42

Chapter 4 Stories Scribbled In Notes

Honor Roll to a Stripper Pole	46
Watching A World Of Misery	49
Foster Care	51
An East Somerville Tragedy	53

Chapter 5 Reflections Of My Mind

Look Through My Eyes	58
Between Me and My Dreams	60
I Hope My Son Won't Be Ashamed	62
The Closest Few	63
Heaven Or Hell	64
Forgive Me	65
My Goodbye Letter	66

Chapter 6 The Lost Pages

Parent Of An Addict	70
No One Could Hear Me Scream	72
Chamber Of Pain	74
Reflections In A Blood Puddle	75
Shedding My Junkie Tears	77

Dedication	79

The Shadow of an Addict

A collection of poetry
by
Matthew Ganem

CHAPTER 1

CONFESSIONS OF A POET

THE DEEPEST ADDICTION IN ME

The pen is my needle
Injecting words of dope
An escape from my everyday evil
A rush that helps me to cope
Paper is packages of Oxy's
Lines I crush in my mind
This wall of writer's blocking me
Snorting gagger's of rhymes
Thoughts of ecstasy I keep
Scribbles inside my hidden fantasies
Trapped by the special K in me
I'm falling in a hole of poetry
Acid tablets wrapped in magic
Hallucinations of the stories I write
Love notes smell like burning plastic
When I place my heart inside a crack pipe
Blunts of ideas burn slower than weed
Self-medicated pain killers
Are stanzas of stress relief
Portraits painted perfect in past pictures
Images of chasing the dragon
Tar stained steps on the tin foil road I walk
Speed balling is my passion
Melting down rock with vinegar thoughts
Shooting up metaphors
For a rush of similes
Expanding what poems explore
The deepest addiction in me
Whatever drug I choose to do
The pen and page combine a perfect fix
Regardless of the feeling I was use to
I never felt a high like this

MY STORY HAS TO BE TOLD

Written in the skyline of Boston
Words that were once too blurry for me
Looking up from the darkness of rock bottom
I kept climbing and eventually I was able to see
The time release coating
I lick off of the best pain killers
Destroy any feeling of my emotion
A reflection of a skeleton in the mirror
An OxyContin love thing began
As the cool thing to do with friends
Snort a half a pill to get jammed
I never envisioned where it would take me in the end
Shirts covered with yellow and green marks
White powder residue on the table
Names soon got tattooed to my heart
After addiction transformed them into angels
No stopping this rolling boulder
As packages started making me money
There wasn't a moment I was sober
But I swore to god I wasn't a junkie
More pills, more crime
The more I got fucked up in the head
A synthetic narcotic left me blind
Invincible, without a care if I ended up dead
Masked armed robberies
Risking parts of my freedom
The time would compare to pennies
Not worth it to go to prison
My habit became too strong
Pushing packs and stick ups weren't enough
Then my lady heroin came along
With a taste of the devils lust
I sold my soul for a filled syringe
Moving death wrapped in plastic
Losing my will to live
As an addict prepared for a casket

Blue lights flashing
Plain clothes hemmed me up
A snitch left me trapped in
The Narco units drug bust
I had to forward my cash to a lawyer
If I had any chance to fight the case
Didn't stop the emotional destroyer
Ready to let my life go to waste
Jail bars didn't stop me
I ran from the court with a ready needle
It all started splitting an Oxy
How could I end up injecting this evil
Violate probation, dodging court dates
Lock ups ready to take me in
Distribution trial had me ready to break
Shooting up an insane amount of heroin
Suicide by needle was the plan
Till I looked beyond the clouds above
On L street beach I was a changed man
My guardian angel wrapped me up with love
The rocky road was ahead of me
With no guarantee I'd make it out alive
Regardless of jail time I grabbed recovery
The Hamilton House was the only reason I survived
Half way to sober or half way to jail
Either way I had to give myself a shot
When my backs against the wall I will prevail
I started my climb to the top
From out the hole
Back on solid ground
I cleansed my scarred soul
Looking at the sky from downtown
It was a cryptic message
With words that were meant for me
"Your life is something you should always cherish"
Thank you my guardian angel, James Slattery
A rebirth from the ashes of yesterday
Carrying my dented halo
The world is gonna hear what I have to say
I have a story that has to be told

I HAVE YOUR NEW ADDICTION

An infection inside these words
My pen is a dirty needle
You can find me on city curbs
Or dark allyways of evil
I scratch that itch
That makes you fiend for more
Agony till the daily fix
Withdrawals feel like death in your core
No Suboxin can avoid the pain
With pinned pupils at a blank page
Tracks blacken each vein
I lock you in a mental cage
My poetry is deadly
Potent enough for a hot shot
The rush creates serenity
Getting high off my lost thoughts
Put the lighter under the spoon
To remove the dirty toxins
Paradise is coming soon
I carry the newest drug supply in Boston
Come get what your disease needs
I'll let you blow a couple lines
An obsession for all color creeds
Once you get high off my rhymes

Push down on the syringe
Injecting a dope poem
This is more than a binge
My words leave your soul broken
Heart bleeding for more
Desperation to read another
Curled up, crying on the floor
Reopening the book cover
Flipping through the pages
Finding the perfect fix
Avoid the sickest stages
By reading it quick
A rush to ease the pain
Opened the healing remedy
When my words touch your brain
Feeding into the addiction of my poetry

A MASKED BANDITS REMORSE

Reappearing in my dreams, my nightmares
Faces that innocently fell into my victim
Tears stain their cheeks, waving a gun in the air
Infecting them with post traumatic stress syndrome
I never thought about the trickledown effect
With masked devils that came through the door
We left them with a memory they'll never forget
After the masked bandits left the store
Heart pumping out of my chest
Clerks struck with the fear of God
We only grabbed the cash then left
Sticking up spots like it was our job
Bandanna's cover a faceless crook
With eyes of a rabid beast
Dignity along with the cash we took
To feed the addict in me
Broken screams in my broken dreams
I hear them yelling at me in my sleep
It's been years since I was a fiend
But the scars I left with them are still deep
Wounds that tore more than flesh
I stripped a part of their normal life
Only to serve a junkies purpose
Of stealing stacks of cash for a trip to paradise

Invincibility found in a little pill
Fear had no place inside
Snorting lines to fulfill
The fact that I was barely alive
Even though I found a way to change
I can't take back what I did
How I inflicted this pain
And rearranged how somebody lived
There's no weight with these words
To the invisible ears, hear this apology
There's no comforting the people I disturbed
But it doesn't take back the fact that I'm sorry

THE PEN IS MY SWORD

When everything stands still
And the world comes to a halt
If it's the disease in me to get killed
Will it be my fault?
My pen is a concealed weapon
Ink ballistics of emotional pain
I got to write my way into heaven
For judgment of my name to change
Mistakes of the past live with me
My remorse can't take them away
Disregard any attempt at sympathy
Apologies can't transform yesterday
Notes of my deepest feelings
Words manipulated together
Its hard to understand how I'm dealing
Living with friends that are gone forever
The sword cuts deep into the page
Opening wounds I tried to hide
Sparking a fire of flames
Igniting the desire inside
Demons in my mind
Crumble beneath my blade
Slaughtered in my lines
That voices of angels made
Thoughts of a prophet
Inside dreams of forgotten youth
Success defies logic
When the devil used a needle to shoot at you

I was never giving a chance
Set up as a kid to fail
Intoxicated by a chemical romance
But I am destined to prevail
I will make it on my own
Without selling my soul to do it
Bare my heart in each poem
With every one of my writings exclusive
Dive into the depths of my work
Swim beneath the channels of my brain
My pen will destroy the curse
That a junkie is the only thing attached to my name

PICTURE ME

Picture me in position better than this
Where reflections of the past disappear
If I could imagine a list
In a moment my life is not clear

Picture me with a wife
A house and a family
Instead of this distorted life
Where it's just my son and me

Picture the athletic ability
Being better than my faded name
Its easy for the naked eye to see
That I've lost a step or two in my game

Picture me not sleeping around
Holding a thousand broken hearts
Finding the queen to my crown
Instead of tearing each girl apart

Picture me making something out of myself
From the rock bottom I hit
Reaching out to those who need help
Still addicted to their fix

Picture me still shooting dope
Married to the needle
Speed balling with coke
Stealing from good people

Picture the path I walk
I've been down this road before
Where suddenly the writing stops
And I can't rhyme the right words any more

Picture never meeting me
So I don't exist in your life
Like I was born in a different city
Would it make you think twice

Picture me as a deadbeat dad
That never supported my kid
Laying in a sleeping bag
Living under the BU bridge

Picture me with fortune and fame
And infinite amounts of money
How much I had to change
For me to strangle recovery

Picture me with a smile
Even after my death
There is still my child
Plus the poems I have left

Picture me with wings in the sky
Holding the memories together
But I will never die
My name will live forever

Picture me in a thousand years
My name etched in stone
Still the boy with tears
Crying in his broken home

Picture me and my shining son
Finding every bit of the good life
I'll never forget where I came from
And what I had to sacrifice

Picture me finally being worth it
After never being good enough
Reaching achievements that serve a purpose
A satisfying feeling for the lives that I touch

NEGATIVITY

I feed off the negativity
Blood pumping anger through my veins
There's no one that wants to dance in the middle with me
After shoveling shit on my name
Yea I'm a poet
Not by title but by body of work
So take my book and close it
If you want to mock me first
You cast a shadow of hatred
Over the steps I take
I leave my heart, body and soul naked
With every piece that I make
I'll be fine if you pay me no mind
Save your two cents for somebody else
With the effort I put in its only a matter of time
For my success to speak for itself
I'm driven to be better than this
While you talk about how I used to use
I make sure there's no opportunity missed
To get my son a new pair of shoes
My hand reaches out for those in need
Pulling them back if they choose to accept
Talking mouths shout about my run ins with police
Back in the day when every crime I came up as a suspect

Today I stand on a different level
With only the scars of the past that remain
I didn't have to sell my soul to the devil
I'd be dead right now if I didn't change
Those wise cracks disappear into thin air
When you whisper in circles I couldn't care less for
Through hell on earth I persevered
It drives me to succeed that much more
I stand on my own two, alone
Never been carried to places I needed to be
Put my life in each poem
I keep feeding off this negativity

CHAPTER 2

BEHIND MY DEEPEST SCAR

NIGHT TERRORS

My nights are so cold
Dreams that feel so real
The devil won't let go
I know just how good it can feel
Dark city streets I walk on
Venom running through my veins
My minds been gone
Since the first RIP tattoo with a name
My fingers wrap around the handle of a gun
Adrenalin produces a natural high
A sick smile I carry for fun
When I start waving a pistol in the sky
I need to feed the disease with OC's
To avoid a sickness killing me inside
I need it more than the air I breathe
Without these pills I'm consumed by suicide
By any means necessary
Regardless if it's by handgun or knife
If they decide not to give these pills to me
I'm ready to take their life
This punk moving major packs
Ten thousand at a time
Bragging about how much cash he stacks
Is getting a meet and greet with my nine
Carrying only a half a clip
Plus one in the chamber
He's gonna be surprised getting pistol whipped
Walking past a stranger
Hitting the ground hard
Blood pouring from his head
Walking through the project courtyard
I could have left him for dead

Dragged him back to his apartment
Duct tape around his ankles and hands
Don't even try to start shit
I'm here for money and the jams
No fear to cover my face
I let him look me in the eyes
He pointed me to the safe
Screaming he doesn't want to die
Forty thousand wrapped by rubber bands
Easily twenty-five thousand Oxycontin pills
I spun around with the gun in my hand
Thinking if it's worth it for him to be killed
Tears streamed down his cheeks
Fear corrupted his body
I woke up from my sleep
With the drip after snorting an Oxy
Running to the bathroom
Splashing water in my face
The disease is in full bloom
I still can't get rid of this taste
Night terrors of a life I left behind
Years have passed but they won't let go
These demons still live in my mind
An addiction infected in my soul

AN OXYCONTIN RELAPSE

The devil is staring back at me
Inside a lifeless form
Living in a distorted reality
My heart is broken and torn
I can't keep my head above water
Drowning beneath crushed pills
Each time I try to quit it gets harder
My search goes unfulfilled for cheap thrills
Boredom sets in cause I lost my friends
Too busy finding a means to get high
So I relapse and go at it again
Kiss my sobriety goodbye
This moment I'm locked in
Standing at the crossroads
Staring at an Oxycontin
Ready to explode
Surely this pain killer
Would be a taste of heaven on earth
I see a stranger in the mirror
Sick and tired of making sober work
Lick the coating then wipe it off
Move it back and forth on a strainer
Make it into a line on the table top
Then snort it all with nothing left to savor

Scratch the itch after getting jammed
Pupils pinned inside my eyes
Oh how I love those eighty milligrams
The second after I get high
Invincibility, I feel like I have no limits
Once I taste the drip
But after the feeling is diminished
I wish I didn't go back to it
It's only gonna get worse
Progressively taking me to a harder drug
If I can't put it down first
I'll be spreading my wings in the clouds above

MY BROWN LADY DISEASE

Struggling with a ball and chain
Wrapped around my brain
I want to call out her name
But the feelings have changed
She used to be my everything
Treated me like a king
Waited on slipping her the ring
Now the heart broken blues I sing
The happiness I remember
Every day we spent together
I swore our love was forever
But our ties had to be severed
Driving a stake through my heart
Leaving dark scar marks
That first day we spent the night in the park
I never wanted us to be apart
Until you broke down my life
Everything I had to sacrifice
For you to end up my wife
Despite the fact you whispered it'd be alright

In sickness and in health
When I needed somebody else
You cut off my outlets for help
With each blow you dealt
A stranger skeleton man
I couldn't understand
When I first had you in my hands
In a few years where I would stand
Beaten and broken
With my whole soul opened
Everything that was stolen
When I let you overtake my emotions
My world revolved around you
The hell on earth you put me through
What did I get myself into
After I had my first taste of you
Jealousy the first second your gone
The sickness with me withdrawn
Animosity for how you did me wrong
You were evil all along

I stare into the temptress's eyes
When I push it inside
A love, hate suicide
The high takes me for a ride
Beauty disappears in dark times
The yearning in the back of my mind
I can't seem to find
When the temptation leaves me blind
I fucking hate you
And everything you do
I see you in my rearview
Years after I told you to screw
Your a trashy whore
That swears you love me more
In that sick little mind of yours
What do you keep bothering me for?
You make me so mad
I disconnected any connection we had
From the pills down to the final bag
I wanted you so bad
Why don't you open up your eyes to see
The fact it took me years to break free
Regardless if your my brown lady disease
There's no love between you and me

RIPPLES OF THE PAST

Staring at an ocean of hope
Watching the past ripple away
I see a time I was controlled by dope
Crying on my darkest day
Needles littered the floor
Ashamed of what I had become
What the hell am I here for
Prepared to die young
When will I serve my earths purpose
Realizing the pain with the love lost
Tracks scar my skins surface
Eyes pinned and bloodshot
In this corner of the room
Shut off from the midday light
I sit here filthy in the nude
Shooting dope until I find the afterlife
This world I live in is so cold
When I get high it's my escape
I let these pills take over my soul
Then the needle let my heart break
On an island of misery
Alone with my mind
Roaming the streets of the city
Trying to get high for the last time
An empty gun in my waste
Pointing a pistol to the brain
Every dollar I can take
To inject venom in my vein
I share a nasty futon
Wearing the same clothes for weeks
Injection spots paint my arms
Demons haunt me in my sleep

The crack of dawn my eyes open
With a sickness infecting me daily
Body screaming for the potion
The only thing that can save me
A monster erupts inside
Transforming into an uncontrollable beast
Trying to swallow me alive
By a progressively invincible disease

Infected through the track marks of my heart
Shooting up is just the foreplay
It promised to me we will never be apart
Leaving me locked inside its doorway
Cuffed and shackled to the ground
Releasing me to score off the dope man
The ball and chain latch around
Once that bag is in my hand
Unforgettable memories drift away with the tide
Relentless waves crash at my feet
All that pain I still hold inside
An agony that's buried in deep
That dark room succumbed to clear skies
Only faint images in my dreams
Today is another day I did not get high
Just another day I'm able to stay clean

FOR THEIR SAKE

Driving at night down streets that I use to roam
Familiar faces are found with their brains blown
It's such a sad sight to see
Watching the infected addiction
Then to remember that used to be me
Standing on the corner in the same condition
Crack pipes and syringes
Bottle caps and cottons
Everything came off the hinges
Once I couldn't afford Oxycontin
I remember that brown fluid
In the cylinder mixing with my blood
The second I pushed down to do it
It was better than making love
If I tied off or not
A rush to the shores of paradise
I pull up to a red light and stopped
To see an old friend clinging to life
Held up by an electrical pole
Drooling from the mouth
Heroin stole that man's soul
He looked like he was about to go out
Close to face planting into the concrete
Suddenly he was standing upright
His nod was deeper than sleep
And his body a skeleton look alike
The devil breathes from his heart
An evil I know too well
I drive pass Foss park
Reliving my days in hell
It's an ugly disease
That has no color creeds
Even if it's in remission in me
It prays for the day it can feed
A pain surges inside my chest
For the lost souls that can't find their way
Drug addiction is merciless
I hope for their sake they get clean one day

MY GATEWAY TO HEROIN

Ahhhhhh!
Curled up in my bed
Wrapped in sweat drenched sheets
This animal screams out in my head
That I need to feed the beast
My supply is empty
And my connect is dry
Brown powder tempts me
I just want to get high
There's not a single pill in the city
For me to avoid this sickness
I feel like I'm dying literally
Addicted to synthetic narcotics
Even if I can find one
What good will it do
I'll still have the runs
I'm used to doing a few
Put them up three at a time
Take off the coating and crush
Make it into one big line
Then snort it for the rush
That's to start my day
Just to get on my feet
Fantasizing where I lay
About an 80 that's so far out of my reach
I can't pick up a pack
To stop this pain
I grabbed my phone fast
It was a call from someone I won't name
Easily placed the thought in my head
That he could score me the quick fix
Weak willed laying on my death bed
I told him to come give me it
The line I sniffed was powder brown
Adding to the epidemic for a Boston, American
The path Oxycontin led me down
Was my gateway to heroin

OVERDOSE

Bleeding my heart out
Laying lifeless on the floor
Everything I had to live without
Had me trying to take that much more
Choking on polluted air
Hollow eyes growing heavy
I'm broken beyond repair
Hoping the reaper forgets me
A cold frosty chill surrounds
The frozen floor crumbles
My heart starts to pound
Each breath is a struggle
Will I find a way to escape
I can't move at all
Its gonna be too late
Even if I had somebody to call
Tears of my last stand
Slide down my blue tinted cheek
Lost the feeling in my hands
Along with my ability to speak
The needle lodged in my vein
Pushed an overpowering rush
A fatal feeling I can never explain
That left my heart crushed
My lungs stopped working
Suffocating the air trapped in my throat
The agony in me stopped hurting
I succumb to an overdose of dope
Eyelids close with the release of my soul
Descending into the clouds above
The disease finally let go
I lost my life in my battle with drugs

RECOVERY'S DISCIPLE

If all it took was my life
I'd sacrifice it twice
To make sure my son was alright
To escape his father's vice
Let me put my heart on a platter
And serve it to those who mattered
I keep working back up that ladder
From the point I was shattered
Open the eyes of the world to see
Drugs disguised what I possibly could be
Survived the beast of a disease
Even with the devil still terrorizing me
Wash the planet of narcotics
Put a bullet in street profits
On this bleak topic
I'll supply supreme logic
Abolish every pain killer
Regardless if it's a new age healer
Weekly prescription fillers
Are the gateway to teenage dealers
I want them to open up my brain
To see if there's a way we can change
How do we start sticking needles in veins
When all I used to do was play games
Infected with addiction
Now my primary mission
Is to make sure my sons never in that position
Facing a date with death or prison
Along with pulling my friends back
The ones we lost to a relapse
This epidemic is stretched across the map
Overdose numbers are climbing fast

I could easily name more than a few
Whose bodies turned blue
Faces I see in my rear view
That keep telling me this is something I gotta do
Getting clean was vital
Call me recoveries disciple
Only an addict by title
Breaking away from the cycle
Cleanse the fabric of my soul
Wash the stains created years ago
All the remorse I can hold
Carrying my dented halo
After burying so many of my friends in the ground
With the grip of the needle almost led me to drown
I want to be remembered right now
As one of the ones who took addiction down
Spark a match and start the fire
Grab a cell phone and get on the wire
Before another family member is found expired
Ink stains where too many names retire
Quit selling death to kids
Before my army will cross the bridge
Rip out the bones from your ribs
And burn down the crack spot where you live
Cemeteries are filled with troubled youths
That took those drugs to shoot
But I'm the living proof
That you don't have to use

Pull those out of the gutters
Before they get buried under
A statistical number
Who die before their father and mother
I've lived to see so many deaths in the streets
To a disease half are scared to speak
Until they're kids an addict and a thief
My wounds are tragically deep
Cause these eyes
Have seen the demise
Of too many lives
I will never be satisfied
Till everyone that died
That I hold a place inside
Be recognized
That they helped someone survive
Death teaches a lesson
That every angel in heaven
Bare wings of protection
To assure their redemption
Ingest these words I write
They might help save a life
Read them tonight
To someone still locked in their vice

YOU GAVE ME BETTER DAYS

The sky, sun and the moon
Through your eyes I see the light
Will this struggle end soon
I'm working for a piece of paradise
You held my hand
Leading me to a better place
Helping me to understand
While always keeping me safe
Darkness clouded my head
Evil engaged my heart
I almost ended up dead
If you didn't pull me out from the dark
Wings wrapped around my body
Healing the wounds that covered my skin
When the rest of the world lost me
You grabbed me and took me back in
The hardest part of my life
I know you carried me through
Bearing a halo and wearing white
I owe the fact that I'm breathing to you
Lifted me up from rock bottom
Addicted to injecting bags of death
You were there when I was gone and forgotten
When only my tattered soul was left
You live within me until I find forever
I love you bro more than words can explain
We will always be together
Thank you my guardian angel James
You didn't turn your back
When everyone left me to die
Led me down the right path
I see your outline in the sky
I'm so grateful for the life that I have
Even though it almost slipped away
Slattery you snatched me up fast
To give me a chance at better days

CHAPTER 3

THE PRISON INSIDE MY HEART

MY CARDS ON THE TABLE

I'm putting my cards on the table
Face up for you to see
There's no need to cut angles
The queen of my heart is what I want you to be
I can't get you off of my mind
Not that it's a bad thing
Wasted enough of my time
With what wrong women bring
By no means do I think I'm perfect
But I know I can keep you with a smile
If you can show me that you're worth it
To slap our names together with a title
Sometimes I can't figure you out
Even though I know I don't have a chance
Trying to see exactly what you're about
In this budding romance
There's only one person I want to talk to
Who can help make a better day
Its no surprise that girl is you
That helps wash all the BS away
I fall to the sheets to sleep
Holding you close to me
You have enough courage to critique
When I ask you for help with my poetry
The kiss of angel lips
A touch of utopia
Slowly letting go of the grip
Of my commitment phobias
If you give something to a woman she makes it better
So I hand over my heart for you to hold
Wrap it inside you're love forever
Just don't ever let me go

UNDER THE MAN ON THE MOON

Under lazy eyes of the man on the moon
I taste your sweet kiss
Entrapped by the scent of your perfume
Softly biting my lower lip
The stars in a midnight sky
Barely visible with the gleam of the city
A morning sun forces the good bye
Of a perfect night having you with me
I watch you close your front door
Before I turn to walk to my truck
You grab me to kiss me once more
Steal one before you slammed the door shut
Time stands still when we're together
Days could pass by and I wouldn't even care
Moments I will always treasure
I only see good things going forward from here
Driving home through Boston
While you fall to the pillow
Your beauty has me locked in
There's no getting caught in the middle
I can't deny my strong attraction
You grabbed a piece of my mind
I fantasize about acts of passion
Actions that will happen in due time
Sometimes its better to take it slow
Wait for the moment to be perfect
I can let what my name dictates go
If you prove to me that you'd be worth it
Trapped by your pretty smile
Mesmerized by the beauty in your eyes
Lost in your city style
I can't hide these feelings building inside
Finally falling asleep into a fantasy land
Only I find you as the girl of my dreams
With a kiss on my lips you take my hand
Silencing when my broken heart screams

CUTS IN MY BROKEN HEART

Curled up in a corner of the room
Heartbroken holding her picture
The pillow hinted with perfume
Writing a note of how I still miss her
Pieces shattered in my chest
Love I let slip away
Only part of my heart left
When she took off on me that day
I wanted this forever
Take me beyond eternity
All I have is what I remember
That we were never meant to be
Though I long to hold her tight
Dreaming of her sweet kiss
She manipulated a hollow life
For me to experience true bliss
Brought me to highs
I never reached before
Then without a goodbye
Left me lifeless on the floor
Her beauty is a ghost
Just a faded memory
Trapped by the one I love the most
Hoping she will return to me eventually

I hear the sorrow in the beat
As agony manifests in the dark
The blue blood that leaks
From the cuts in my broken heart
I need to be put back together
Disassembled from the truth
Each part of me you severed
While I was screaming out for you
I need you to breathe
The air you sucked out of my lung
My love, you were my disease
Infected in me to die young
Flames ignite the tear stained note
As I pick myself up off the ground
Her love grabbed me by the throat
But I'll never let a woman break me down

FALLING INTO FANTASIES

Will this life ever be complete
Till I find the perfect girl for me
It seems every woman I meet
Will fade away eventually
The fire of lust in beautiful eyes
That stare inside mine
Prepared to be paralyzed
Controlled by the mind
My heart has been broken
Reincarnated with evil
Half of it was stolen
By the demon of needles
I lend my body for tonight
Never promising tomorrow
Breaking through the morning light
I leave behind my sorrow
Physical acts release emotional pain
Feelings I hide deep inside
I'm still scarred by the names
Of those who buried me alive

A fortress protects my chest
Listen for my soft heart beat
There's only a part of it left
So the sound of the beat is weak
An angry man with an old soul
I carry around heavy burdens
But every girl that I hold
I turn and leave them hurting
Solitary confinement without prison
Alone in my own home
I put myself in this position
Expressing my troubles in a poem
Maybe one day
I can pull the beauty out of my dreams
So I fall asleep and drift away
Hoping she will fall into one of my fantasies

CHAPTER 4

STORIES SCRIBBLED IN NOTES

HONOR ROLL TO A STRIPPER POLE

I sit in the center of town
Around the corner from a catholic school
Before everything in her life broke down
She was smart, intelligent and beautiful
A uniform she wore with a short skirt
Carrying the innocence of an angel
Everyday she did her homework
And sat with her family at the dinner table
Graduated on the honor roll
Prepared for the new challenges of college
The chapter changed as her story was told
She left the path of so much promise
Temptation of fast money
Brought along an unmatched excitement
She was living her life hungry
Starving to be something more than a student
The lights turned on
She was the star of the stage
Dancing in a thong
Earning every dollar she made
Gyrating to the music
Bouncing her ass on laps
Financially, she didn't have to do it
But money never came in this fast
A college dropout
Fitting stacks of cash in her purse
Had the ability to choose a different route
But stripping quenched her thirst

Planting her naked body
Inside the mind of men
Once she was introduced to Oxy's
That woman was never the same again
Wrapped up in a dollar bill
Along with a man's number
She took that little pill
The reason everything went under
Stripping, sniffing every night
Getting high before her routine
She was living the good life
Trapped in a cracked in half dream
Unable to dance she moved up to dope
Quickly moving from lines to needles
Lost every bit of hope
Falling into the wrong crowd of people
Every time she tries to shoot a bag of brown
She can't find a vein
I still sit in that center of town
Where her innocent youth remains
Off to college, a catholic school girl
That transformed into a stripper
Infected by an evil world
Oh how bad her family misses her

Car filled with syringes
Still trying to strip for cash
In her mind it was another one of her binges
Only she didn't realize how long it would last
Tracks she tries to hide
Standing before the bright lights
In front of a whole room of guys
She falls during her song twice
Laying by the stripper pole
Barely breathing
Its how her story gets told
Clinging to her life was a good enough reason
She managed to turn it all around
Its five clean years that had passed
Walking up to me in that center of town
But you could never tell the story of her past
A smile on her face
We been through the same storm
She grabs me to embrace
Happy that she was reborn
She kissed me on the cheek
Then kept walking forward in life
 Fought off a disease
 And left me with a story to write
 Endings are usually met with overdoses
 Bigger numbers of gruesome statistics
 Success stories strengthen my focus
 She overcame being a dope addict

WATCHING A WORLD OF MISERY

Bullets flying by the stoop I sit on
Destroying the broken world around me
I've been in this bad dream for so long
Take a listen as I describe what surrounds me
Poison packages in hand to hands
From corner hustler passed to an addict
Escalade driven by the projects dope man
Goons and guns is how the guy lasted
Chrome wheels ignite the night
While kids dream of being in his shoes
Pills, brown powder and white
Fill up his plate with food
I watch masked armed bandits
Guns drawn in the shadows
Execute exactly how they planned it
Leaving the dope man tied up by the trash barrels
The perfect heist
Product, cash, guns and a car to chop
I guess the money wasn't worth his life
Or the respect that he lost
Yet I turn to look down the street
At a kid that's starving to eat
Stab a man in the cheek
For trying to take a piece
Blood puddles around his face
Emt's didn't make it in time
Police tape off the place
A chalk stencil of that mans outline
Blue lights bounce off the buildings
As everyone watches from their window
Another unnecessary killing
From a fatherless child that was never taught to grow

He looked up to the wrong people
Making fast cash with drugs
Older kids started fronting him bags of evil
That was the reason that addict lay in a pool of blood
A nosy neighbor seen what happened
Passing along the kids identity
Then a news conference with the captain
Has that teenager heading to a penitentiary
Spending the rest of his life in jail
Moments before he had passed by my stoop
On his way to make a forty dollar crack sale
He killed the man for trying to take his loot
Its a brick jungle where the good die young
The bad grab one way tickets to prison
The strong take it with a hand gun
Before cascades of bullets hit them
Single mothers do it on their own
Forced by the actions of a dead beat
I got thrown out of my broken home
That's why I'm positioned on this street
With crack pipes and kingpins
Empty weed baggies and needles
Where stabbings happen every weekend
And prostitutes pocket loot of deprived people
XXX spots and neighborhood liquor stores
With broken beer bottles by the entrance
Sides stained by graffiti wars
And murals of angels that made it to heaven
Cops try to control the city
Where criminals out number each one by sixty
Predators prey on misery
Injecting my poetry with the things I see
Walking back up the steps
Happy to live another day in my life
Lay down on the couch in the projects
After I capture my world when I write

FOSTER CARE

An attention deprived child
Hides alone in his room
In silence he stays there for awhile
Away from what his mother turns into
On the couch in the parlor
Her eyes roll into the back of her head
Some nights its harder
To tell if she's dead
Food stamps and welfare
Government benefits recipient
But the fridge is bare
From a parents negligence
She turns the assistance
Into filling up her needles
Then to avoid dope sickness
Sells herself to people
Sleeping with a random man for cash
Her child inside their home
Inhaling second hand crack
He feels the side effects of getting stoned

A dope addict and a bad mother
Would have sold her son to get high
He found her frozen blue under covers
With a lifeless look in her eyes
Laying with her body for days
He cried eternal tears of pain
Didn't want his mommy to go away
Screaming her name when the police came
The forbidden fruit of drug use
Left that kid without a family
The agony walking in his shoes
While he visits his mom at the cemetery
She chose dope over her son
Leaving behind a rose with his tears
He will always miss his mom
As he enters into the custody of foster care

AN EAST SOMERVILLE TRAGEDY

Living inside houses on different sides of the street
But divided by a distinctive line
A line that meant there could never be peace
The battle had been raging for a long time
Handsome and covered by tattoos
Jimmy, the leader of that part of the city
Running around with a large crew
Involved with criminal activity
The place was in Somerville
Staring across at Charlestown
Each trying to control distribution of pills
Turning the area into a battle ground
Fights, stabbings and a few missed shots
Plus a couple of ICU visits
The violence never stopped
Bad blood has boiled for their entire existence
Johnny ran the group of Townies
A former gold glove boxer
Convicted with a few assault and battery's
And a smooth, slick talker
Their personal beef stretched from high school
Fighting after football games
Then at Good Times playing pool
Johnny walked up and stabbed James
In revenge Jimmy blew up John's car
Not that he ever found the proof
They both walk around with scars
From unfortunate acts that enemies do
Sitting back on the top of his stoop
Jimmy sees a beauty struggling with groceries
A sexy girl and her smile was cute
He walked over and told her to hand one of those bags over to me
She quickly obliged with an immediate attraction
Walking her down the wrong side of the street
If a Townie saw them it would set off a chain reaction
But James was never scared of beef

Each step they walked closer
Till they stopped at the front door of Johnny's house
She was Johns cousin from Oklahoma
And his mother was helping her out
It was her first semester at Boston University
And she couldn't afford to live in the dorms
He offered to take her to dinner and a movie
She wrote her info on the back of a job application form
Adriana and her number surrounded by a heart
He put the paper in his pocket as he walked back home
The man fell in love with her from the start
Fighting with himself for hours to call her phone
Finally he did in the afternoon of the next day
She was gorgeous with green eyes and dark hair
They decided to make a date for this Friday
Taking her to Vinny's then to see The Fighter in Revere

That date put them together for the next few months
When a plot formulated to get the Townies supply
Some information came up from a drunk at lunch
Who was an uncle for one of Johnny's top guys
Sold out the whole plan for a few bucks
And had Jimmy flying up Main street
His crew behind him in stolen trucks
Looking for a bigger piece to eat
The Townies weren't ready
When they kicked down the front door
If they were it could have been deadly
But Jimmy planned out the perfect score

There goes the Charlestown drug trade
Somerville had taken over
It left Johnny enraged
Gathering up every one of his foot soldiers
Back to the stash house on Pearl
They unloaded the product they just took
Jimmy had a date with his girl
Dinner at Strega's was booked
Hopped in his car and headed for his house
Pulled up as Adriana was crossing the road
He gave her a hug as Johnny rolled up with guns out
Jimmy didn't know till he heard the barrel explode
She fell to the ground with a bullet in her back
Johnny realizes he just shot his family
Jimmy pulls the trigger of the thirty-eight in his grasp
Slaying his enemy with no mercy
The dividing line connected with blood
As James fights back the tears in his eye
Holding the one that he loved
Although she is no longer alive
Blue lights from cop cars pull onto the scene
Closing the chapter of another love story
Hand cuffs are reality of this dream
Ending this East Somerville tragedy

CHAPTER 5

REFLECTIONS OF MY MIND

LOOK THROUGH MY EYES

Stop and wait a second
Close your eyes to open your mind
I will paint a picture in a direction
That if you opened your eyes they'd be mine
Take a vision from me
Walking miles wearing my shoes
Look through my eyes to see
What it's like for me to replace you
Watch your friends succumb to drugs
The same drugs you snort or shot
Find hallways full of blood
When you come out of apartments lost
See people you know in the streets
Huddled in the dark disguised as zombies
Infected with an addiction for a disease
That come out of the shadows to harm me
Be there when my parents split
My father took off on his own
Feel your face get hit
Cause you still lived in that broken home
Watch Oxycontin take over your life
Pills become your sick obsession
Not knowing if you make it through the night
Or if you're gonna wake up in heaven
See the suicide of your best friend
An image burned in my brain forever
Always be considered less than
Each day I wanted to give up and surrender

Push through the hardest parts
When I lost the will to live
Close your eyes after dark
Huddled up sleeping under a bridge
Never see your family
Too busy coping dope
Become numb to reality
By giving up hope
Reach up from the depths of rock bottom
Without a single soul there to help
Come to the point you run out of options
And take a good hard look at yourself
Resiliency is an understatement
Its not in me to be a quitter
I'm not a product of my placement
I'd be evil no matter where I was delivered
Coming back from the dead
Looking at a time I was barely alive
Unable to escape my head
Do you understand how hard it is to survive
Take a vision from me
Walking miles in my shoes
Look through my eyes to see
If you could walk down the same avenues

BETWEEN ME AND MY DREAMS

Tossing and turning in the sheets
Another sleepless night
My body feels broken and weak
Pushing towards a better life
Bags weigh down my eyes
Stress is found in my bones
I keep reaching for the prize
Beyond points of the unknown
Darkness between me and my dreams
A black hole of unrest
Will I silence when my demons scream
Climbing the ladder to success
Tormented souls of yesterday
Former friends I can't recognize
Transform from the words I say
Lifting their spirit to survive
The grass is greener on the other side
But I'm trapped in a concrete city
Travel down the tracks on a train ride
Through the darkness that's with me
Black clouds circle my head
Pain infects my heart
I remember every word she said
Right before she ripped me apart
Inside a battle rages
I was born for war
Locked my insanity in bracelets
Chained the beast to the floor

Hide behind my devil eyes
An evil trails my shadow
I live under darker skies
Blacked out from a thousand arrows
Cupids army of hate
The baby of love is gone
I watch countless heartbreak
As more time moves along
The vessel in my chest is made of stone
Rock hard, never to be broken
I can make it through the rest of my life alone
If the pieces I have left are never stolen
Ice pumps through my arteries
Frozen cold focused on my goals
Drive and determination is a part of me
I will make it past any obstacle on this road
At rock bottom I thought my life was over
Till I built up the courage to make it out
Now I feel success creeping in closer
By choosing to go a different route
This darkness that separates me
Signals a symbol centered in pain
The ghost shadow of an adversary
That stands before me without a name
With every line leading to an escape
Working towards the promise land
Each step I take with blind faith
Hoping to become a better man

I HOPE MY SON WON'T BE ASHAMED

I wonder in future years
Will the opinion of me change
Once my son hears
How his father used to be deranged
The past will not be hidden
Honesty with the questions he asks
I will be open with my addiction
So he knows how everything can crumble fast
From the crimes I used to commit
To the drugs I used to ingest
How quickly I became a dope addict
With the evil I used to inject
I hope he isn't ashamed
When he looks me in the eye
That he carry the last name
Of his father that used to get high
If I could turn back time
I would smack some sense into me
Only it would destroy the ultimate design
That brought a miracle to my family
The road down recovery way
Where I met the mother of my son
Would disappear if I could go back into yesterday
And change the mistakes I made when I was young
If I never struggled with addiction
I wouldn't be the father of my little man
When he's in the right position to listen
I will tell him when he's old enough to understand
Maybe he will look at me different
Maybe his thoughts will still be the same
I carry fear until we reach that moment
I never want to lose the love of my Christian James
Mistakes get made there's no changing that
I have to live with what happened in my life
So I will confront my past when he asks
I just hope the end outcome will be alright

THE CLOSEST FEW

Lost in the vision of one
Eyes of a thousand stand beside me
Those I lost that were too young
Reach out from beyond the cemetery
Wings spread out
Deflecting the danger I face
Ghosts that are there when it counts
To help keep me safe
Loyalty is a fading trend
In this city of cut throats
I trust in my few close friends
That I love the most
When I face the faces of a thousand strong
By my side they stand tall
Whether I'm right or wrong
They would be there to stop my downfall
Years pass by
And some things change
More angels fly
Losing the life of another name
It means nothing to have a thousand friends
But not one you can count on in a time of need
I'll take the ones who will be there in the end
When a thousand enemies are coming after me
Side by side they stand without fear
Ready to take on blood thirsty adversity
I love my friends that would stand there
When outnumbered by more than thirty
A place in my heart for those who remain true
Stick together for the tribulations we go through
To my friends, brothers, the closest few
I love every one of you

HEAVEN OR HELL

Tangled in the afterlife of resurrection
Breaking point between heaven and hell
My body is pulled in both directions
One hand held by an angel, one by the devil
My skin is melted from the wrong I've done
Sins I could never be forgiven for
I see the faces of those that died young
Fighting against the devils roar!
He pulls me towards the fire
Flames that dance before my eyes
While the angels take me higher
Trying to lift me through the sky
The war between good and evil
Judgment for the mistakes I made
Or how I affected certain people
Manipulating the words I say
My devil horns hold up my halo
As blood drips down my forehead
Falling towards a world inside a volcano
But I wanted to find paradise past my deathbed
Tears stain the skin of my face
I had so much more to live for
Please take me away from this place
Let me spread my wings and soar
The fire in hell clashed with the heavens above
A battle to see who takes control of my soul
Wrapped in an guardian angel's love
All the evil in my heart was let go
Released from the devils grip
Ascending to the clouds of eternity
The angels that helped me drift
Were the best friends that lived through me

FORGIVE ME

Forgive me for the wrong in my life
The mistaken choices I made
Even if I tried to make it right
Some feelings will never fade
Forgive me for being a bad son
I took for granted both parents
The broken home I was thrown from
After how I acted during the end of their marriage
Forgive me for the trouble in school
I tarnished my last name
Broke the rules thinking it was cool
Only I inflicted my family with pain
Forgive me for destroying lives
Selling addiction in plastic
There's still nights I cry
Haunted by familiar faces in caskets
Forgive me for becoming a junkie
A progression that was easy
To have everyone that loved me
End up leaving me
Forgive me for the hearts in my hand
Pieces of women that I've stolen
Hurting you was never my plan
I'm scared to leave myself open
Forgive me for my trust issues
There was a time when I was all alone
Walk in my drug addict shoes
When I had no place to call my home
Forgive me for not being a better friend
I try to be the best one that I can be
Hoping I will be good enough in the end
For everybody to be proud of me
Forgive me for everything of my past
So I can only look forward to the future
Forgiveness is easy for me to ask
Only I should have apologized sooner

MY GOODBYE LETTER

What if this was the last breath
The last second on earth
I couldn't walk past death
When the reaper grabs me first
How would I be remembered
In small groups of old friends
If this was my goodbye letter
What would I say at the end
I hope my friends and family
Let my spirit live longer than my name
Words that still breathe the life in me
Please smile, they just took away the pain
The burdens of stress is gone
This weight has been lifted
I'll always love you mom
I sincerely ask for your forgiveness
There's no better man than you dad
Even though our flaws are the same
I never meant to turn out this bad
But I hope your opinion of me has changed
Ashley, I love you my beautiful little sis
The perfect person in a world so cold
When I was broke you helped fix
The damage done to a poisoned soul
I want my memory to be happy
No tears when I cross to the other side
Bring laughter to my cemetery
Or I will wash away the tears from your eyes

Everything I ever wrote
Will still be here beyond my dying day
Echoes of my ghost
Heard after the dust from my bones blow away
Christian, I love you more than words can explain
I just hope you are proud to have me as a father
The mistakes I made were in vein
If you don't learn how to cope when life gets harder
I tried my very best to put you in a better position
While leaving you a personal description of myself
You are the one person I am truly missing
The love you gave me I couldn't get from anybody else
I spread my wings perched atop my cloud
Joining the rest of friends that fell in deaths tangles
When you think of me now I hope you're proud
Christian I'm always with you as your guardian angel

CHAPTER 6

THE LOST PAGES

PARENT OF AN ADDICT

With my head down
Pain weighs upon my heart
Every time you come around
I'm broken apart
I've loved you since you opened your eyes
When I held you in my hands
Some nights I wonder if your still alive
I'm trying to do the best that I can
You're a shadow of the child I raised
Oblivious to the fact that I know
I have nightmares standing at your grave
While I watch you physically die slow
Everyone tells me I need to give you tough love
Turn my back and stop being your crutch
I help enable your abuse on drugs
By always trying to do too much
Nodding off in the middle of conversations
Locking yourself in the bathroom for hours
Taking off after one day as a detox patient
Finding your needles left behind in the shower
This madness needs to stop
You've become a stranger to me
You're either gonna be locked in a box
Or in danger of ending in the cemetery
I don't want to lose you
But you are spiraling lower and lower
It's a decision I can't force you to do
I just want you to get sober

Those so called friends you defend
Only care about themselves
They will take off on you in the end
If you overdosed and needed some help
I've had dreams of you in a bath tub
Left behind to die
A bad combination of drugs
Why do you have to get high?
I remember you as an innocent kid
Now I dread the nights you're not home
This is no way for you to live
It breaks my heart thinking about you when I'm alone
You look like death
With black pockets below your eye sockets
Everybody knows you're a mess
And it's killing me I can't do a thing to stop it
Sleeping in the same clothes as yesterday
Sprawled out on the couch
It hurts in the worst way
I'd rather you be high in my house
At least then I would know where you are
And I can be there to help you
This is so hard
Watching the transformation you're going through
I know I'll wake up and something will be missing
Cash, lab top or maybe my check book
I don't have the heart to send you to prison
My baby, you're not cut out to be a crook
Anxiety kicks in every time my phone rings
Wondering if this will be that unwanted call
A parent of an addict with the depression that brings
Carrying the burden that I let my child fall
Please just find the courage to get into recovery
I don't want your fate to be like so many others
Losing you would be the death of me
And I know you don't want to do that to me and your mother
Sitting up on another restless night
Hoping for a miracle
Someone please protect my kids life
The love for my child is unconditional

NO ONE COULD HEAR ME SCREAM

Standing in a room of sorrow
I gracefully move without being seen
Lost my shot of seeing tomorrow
Unable to wake up from this dream
Black dresses and suits with ties
Tears spilling from the cheeks of friends
Since birth is a guarantee to die
I never been scared to face death in the end
Pictures from yesterdays taped to poster board
While people years removed remember way back when
Echoes of my name float around the funeral home floor
Leaving the lips of people I'm never gonna see again
Caked on make up, I can barely recognize myself
With the essence of my soul still breathing
It hurts when I reach out at someone to help
But I can't stop their painful feeling
Friends kneeling beside me
My family lined up next to the casket
Crossing to the other side this young was unlikely
But I still can't believe how long I lasted
Looking over the shoulder of the priest
While he speaks about the passing of God's child
It's a shame through the years I lost belief
As he keeps flipping through the pages of the bible
I always dreamed about making it to heaven
Forgiveness granted for the mistakes that I made
Consistently failed the test of my life lessons
That I fear will haunt me on my judgment day

I show a sinner's remorse
Sitting in the middle of my own wake
Watching two parents that were divorced
My father wiping tears off my mother's face
Crying eyes break the silence
Heartbreak consoled in the arms of comfort
Each person giving their condolence
In an attempt to help them move forward
Open coffin but my eyes are closed
Never to see the light of day
I wish there was a way for everyone to know
That I love them even if it's something too late to say
Old photographs beginning with the cradle
A timeline of still frames
I spread bloody wings as I transform into an angel
But I couldn't figure out how to kill the pain
I built a lifetime of regrets
Caused many love ones to suffer
Now I step into the darkness
The fingers of death pulling me under
Broken wings unable to fly
A soul I could never wash clean
Without a voice I try to say goodbye
But no one in the room could hear me scream

CHAMBER OF PAIN

Maniac mental state
Alone in my own mind
Demons taking up rental space
I feel their fingertips down my spine
Different voices screaming in my head
Evil whispers, twisting me to sin
The truth in every word that I said
I swear to god I'm never going back again
Open the eyes inside each thought
To look at the subliminal message
I was born when a devil and an angel crossed
Created inside of the wreckage
Friends became strangers and changed
Turning their back to tear me apart
Restrained in my chamber of pain
Protecting the cracked part of my heart
Backing myself into a corner
Away from fake smiles on familiar faces
Infected with a mental health disorder
Insanity building in unfamiliar places
The people in my life I held close
Always there for someone in need
Disrespected when I needed someone the most
Alone in a hole with nobody there for me
My pen developed into my only friend
Releasing my built up aggression
I know I'd be lonely in the end
Spilling my emotions in notebook confessions
Every word I write is reality
I don't sugarcoat the problems of my past
Trapped inside my own agony
Stranded on the path of an outcast

REFLECTIONS IN A BLOOD PUDDLE

Patiently passing progress reports on life
From situations I've seen with my own eyes
The pen is an extension of me when I write
Describing how hard it is out there to survive
Death, pain, misfortune and struggle
Lust, greed, jealousy and envy
Staring at a reflection through a blood puddle
At the face of an angel that was mortally set free
Children lost in the anarchy of an adult
Trapped youth inside a sacred heart
Living in this cold world is so difficult
When temptations touched us from the start
The glory of a fast buck
Enticed by the luxury of being rich
Birth can be a stroke of bad luck
On the poor, poverty end of the stick
Money makes the world turn
Cash has an image that it can take the pain away
A disguised devil will let your soul burn
If it's materialistic wishes when you kneel down to pray
Concrete cities secluded communities
Concentrated with no income households
Teenagers look up to the people on T.V.
Rap stars and gangsters helping a criminal to grow
Green is the color of greed
Project dreams of hustling an escape
Emotions are quicker to bleed
Drugs destroy the potential to be great
Selling to the disease infected
Holding corner territories
Misery wrapped in plastic
Pumping pleasure for those with the poor me's
That little baggie of powder or pills
Break away from the reality of it all
In the midnight hour a coward kills
Withdrawals are fatal when the drug calls

Murder on the hands of an addict
Crack stole the man's conscience
Inhale each hit of the madness
Blood money in his pockets
A friend I knew for a life time
Staring with eyes of death
Has a chalk stenciled outline
On the corner where his body rests
Blue lights ricocheted through a sky with no stars
Tears for a fallen angel stream down my cheek
Pain infused on the boulevard
Another one of my friends dead in the streets
Uneducated in business
But masters in their own mind
Pipe dreams like the skies the limit
Often end up with their bodies left behind
Shoe boxes filled with re-up money
Small safes holding twenty grand
If they stopped supplying junkies
They could triple their profit as an educated man
Invest in their drive for cash
Putting their head in a book
Pay attention in class
Instead of ending up dead as a crook
Learn to better yourself
Without polluting people
College is an easy way to help
Get away from the corner evil
Those profits are nice
For the small window you can sell
There are only two options in that life
Death or a happy home in a cell
Intolerance to believe in something more
Blindfolded beyond his drug hustle
He was just a kid, weeks before he turned twenty four
Tangled in the vines of the concrete jungle
Police officers zip my boy in a body bag
Stiff, soulless and frozen cold
Childhood memories is all have
Sitting on the steps as I watch him go

SHEDDING MY JUNKIE TEARS

Standing in front of small circles
Speaking out of past memories
Problems too hard to work through
When it's only the reflection and me
Retracing the steps of yesterday
Times in my life I screwed up
Help me get through the rest of today
I feel like I've had too much
Things are just so hard now
I can't find enjoyment being sober
Even if it makes my parents proud
Give me a pain-killer instead of this Coca-Cola
As a matter of fact, give me a rail of coke
At this point a relapse
Is only a relapse if I do dope
I never even liked the white powder
Intoxicated by prescription pills
Let me muster up the willpower
Cause this boredom kills
Being broke doesn't help
I can't afford a pack of cigarettes
Where is everybody else
I could never take a day off
Now I sit in my pity pot
Staring till the walls start closing in
When will this mental madness stop?
I really don't want to do dope again
Truly, I am a bad day away from the needle
Speaking honestly from the heart
Isolated myself from sober people
To let my addiction boil in the dark
Maybe I am glorifying the drug
Placing heroin on a pedestal
Forget about the plunge
Where I transformed into a junk box criminal
I'm still a struggling addict
Impatiently waiting, each month I grab my chip
Dealing with my reservations

I want to get high
That's why I'm standing before you
Speaking about the reasons why
And the struggles I go through
Today I don't have to use
It's a choice I'm free to make
I'm not willing to lose
For a mistake of not playing the tape
Those hours waiting on a dealer
That said they'd be there in five minutes
Not looking at the image in the mirror
Loading up those syringes
Bathrooms of gas stations
Places for me to stick a vein
Violated terms of probation
Dodging the date to be shackled in chains
Friend's eyes closed in caskets
Shedding my junkie tears
Any injection could be tragic
Nightmares of me laying in there
Breaking into an abandoned house
Getting high with my so called friends
I could have overdosed on the couch
And they would take off on me in the end
Turned my back on my family
So I can live in these streets
Where the drugs stole my sanity
To give birth to my disease
Withdrawals crippled me
A sickness inside I could never forget
God grant me the serenity
To understand what's hard to accept
I'm a drug dependent person
That breaks out in destruction when I get high
Recovery will stop working
If I don't remember the reasons why
I have an incurable disease
Infected in me for the rest of my life
Sometimes I need to vent to believe
Everything will eventually be alright

Dedication

This book is dedicated to Christian James Ganem first and foremost, the reason anything in my life gets done, I love you my son. I want to thank Iggy Gibson for everything he has done for me, helping me to open doors and expand the poetry that I write into something visual for the world to see. With his help, my writing has reached a larger audience and opened doors to new opportunities for me, thank you. I want to thank all my friends and family that support me and help with whatever I need, it means everything to me, I love everyone of you, I am very grateful for the people in my life. Everyone that reads my stuff, watches the videos, buys the book and reaches out to me as a fan, thank you guys for being in my corner, it keeps pushing me to do more, thank you!

Rest In Peace to Danny Nunes, James Slattery, Stephen Pacheco, Michael Sparks and Joseph Ganem, I will carry every one of your names until my dying day.

Thank you to Doug Sparks for always being there for me while I try to make a name for myself as a poet. People have tried to crush my dreams by telling me I have no chance to go anywhere with this and the roadblocks I had to face, you have always been in my corner helping me to get this project off the ground.

I want to give a special thanks to Jasen Sousa of J-Rock Publishing, Erin Marie Daley Gover of Oxy-Watchdog.com and James Mcgilvary of the radio show Doctors Prescriptions, Deadly Addictions, who are huge advocates against addiction and have given me opportunities to spread my work into different states and communities.